WHAT TO DO WHEN THE STORM COMES

NATALIE C. CHUBBS

Around HIM
PUBLISHING

Copyright © 2015 Natalie C. Chubbs
Published by Around H.I.M. Publishing

For publishing information, address:
Around His Image Marketing and Publishing
5 W. Hargett Street, Raleigh, NC 27601
www.aroundhim.com
info@aroundHim.com

All rights reserved, including the right of reproduction in whole or in part in any form. No part of this publication may be stored in any retrieval system or transmitted in any form or by electronic, mechanical, photocopying, recording or otherwise without the written permission of the publisher.

Manufactured & printed in the
United States of America

ISBN 978-1511665933

Table of Contents

Foreword & Acknowledgements 1

Spreading Awareness 3

   Dystonia 3

   Hemiplegic Migraines 4

   Vasovagal Syncope 7

Chapter 1: When Things Fell Apart 9

Chapter 2: What's Happening to Me? 16

Chapter 3: Fighting to Find Myself 32

Chapter 4: Regrouping 41

Chapter 5: Hitting Rock Bottom 47

Chapter 6: The Break Through 61

Chapter 7: Turning Disappointment into an opportunity 64

Closing Remarks 70

About The Author 73

WHAT TO DO WHEN THE STORM COMES

Foreword & Acknowledgements

"And the God of all grace, who called you to his eternal glory in Christ, after you have suffered a little while, will himself restore you and make you strong, firm and steadfast." 1st Peter 5:10

This journey started for me and my family in February 2010 and is ongoing. It has been a road that has consisted of many twists and turns, imbedded with multiple trials and tribulations. My hope is that I will encourage someone by telling my story. By sharing how faith, prayer, steadfastness, and self-advocacy have led me to triumph, I hope that others will be inspired to pursue answers to the health issues that are eluding them no matter how daunting the task may be. There is an answer to your questions. America's healthcare system-today is driven more by insurance companies than consumers. We have to take an active approach in our healthcare process. We need to be empowered in more ways than one. This is a peek into my self-discovery, how I navigated finding a diagnosis, and how God strengthened my faith in him during the process.

I would like to thank my husband, children, my mother, father, mother-in-law, father-in-law, sister-in-law, my two younger brothers and my true friends (you know who you are) for being there for me through these past few years of trials and tribulations! I would also like to thank my dear friend Kimberly Curtis Shoulars for her feedback and helping to ensure that this book would be all God would have it to be! May God continue to bless each and every one of you!

Spreading Awareness

"Wisdom is the principal thing; therefore get wisdom: and with all thy getting get understanding." Proverbs 4:7 (KJV)

Facts that you need to know about the diagnosis by which I am affected:

Dystonia
What is Dystonia?

Dystonia is a movement disorder. Dystonia is characterized by persistent or intermittent muscle contractions causing abnormal, often repetitive, movements, postures, or both. The movements are usually patterned and twisting, and may resemble a tremor. Dystonia is often initiated or worsened by voluntary movements, and symptoms may "overflow" into adjacent muscles. Although, there are several forms of Dystonia and the symptoms may outwardly appear quite different. The element that all forms share is the repetitive, patterned, and often twisting involuntary muscle contractions. Dystonia is a chronic disorder, but the vast majority of Dystonias do not impact cognition, intelligence, or shorten a person's life span.

Dystonia is classified by:

1. Clinical characteristics (including age of onset, body distribution, nature of the symptoms, and asso-

ciated features such as additional movement disorders or neurological symptoms)

2. Cause (which includes changes or damage to the nervous system and inheritance).

Doctors use these classifications to guide diagnosis and treatment.

There are multiple forms of Dystonia, and dozens of diseases and conditions may include Dystonia as a symptom. Dystonia may affect a single body area or be generalized throughout multiple muscle groups. Dystonia affects men, women, and children of all ages and backgrounds. Estimates suggest that no fewer than 300,000 people are affected in the United States and Canada alone. Dystonia causes varying degrees of disability and pain, from mild to severe. There is presently no cure, but multiple treatment options exist and scientists around the world are actively pursuing research toward new therapies.
www.dystonia-foundation.org

Hemiplegic Migraines
What is Hemiplegic Migraine?

Hemiplegic migraine is a rare type of headache. It's also one of the most serious and potentially debilitating migraine headaches.

What Is a Hemiplegic Migraine Headache?

There are several types of migraine. One major group is called <u>migraine with aura</u>. Hemiplegic migraine is a severe subtype of this group.

Migraine is a complex neurological disorder. It generally includes headaches, but not always. Before the actual headache <u>pain</u> of a migraine, a host of other symptoms may be present that serve as warning signs that a migraine is coming. These early symptoms, called auras, include temporary disturbances in one or more functions:
- Vision
- Muscle control and body sensations
- Speech and language
- Hearing

For most migraine sufferers who have aura, the visual disturbances are the most common symptom. But for people with hemiplegic migraine, muscle weakness and paralysis can be so pronounced and extreme that they cause a temporary, <u>stroke</u>-like paralysis on one side of the body. This paralysis on one side of the body is called hemiplegic.

What Are the Symptoms of Hemiplegic Migraine Headaches?

Hemiplegic migraine symptoms often start in childhood. For some people, they disappear in adulthood. The stroke-like symptoms can range from worrisome to debilitating. Migraines are unpredictable and unique to each person. You may have a hemiplegic migraine headache with extreme pain and minor paralysis one month. Then, the next attack might bring extreme paralysis without much headache pain at all.

Symptoms of hemiplegic migraine include:
- Severe, throbbing pain, often on one side of the head
- Pins-and-needles feeling, often moving from the hand up the arm
- Numbness on one side of the body, which can include the arm, leg, and/or one side of the face
- Weakness or paralysis on one side of the body
- Loss of balance and coordination
- Visual aura, such as seeing zigzag lines, <u>double vision</u>, or blind spots
- Language difficulties, such as mixing words or trouble remembering a word
- Slurred speech
- Dizziness or vertigo
- Nausea and vomiting
- Extreme sensitivity to light, sound, and smell
- Confusion
- Decreased consciousness or coma

With hemiplegic migraine, the aura can be more severe and last longer than with other types of migraine with aura. Symptoms usually last from five minutes to one hour. While rare, some people gradually develop long-lasting difficulty with movement and coordination.

Vasovagal Syncope
Vasovagal syncope (vay-zoh-VAY-gul SING-kuh-pee) is one of the most common causes of fainting. Vasovagal syncope occurs when the body overreacts to certain triggers, such as the sight of blood or extreme emotional distress.

The vasovagal syncope trigger causes a sudden drop in heart rate and blood pressure. This leads to reduced blood flow to the brain resulting in a brief loss of consciousness.

Vasovagal syncope is usually harmless and requires no treatment. However, it's possible to injure oneself during a vasovagal syncope episode. Also, a doctor may recommend tests to rule out more-serious causes of fainting, such as heart disorders.

Before fainting due to vasovagal syncope, a person may experience some of the following:
- Skin paleness

Finding Strength Through Adversity

- Lightheadedness
- Tunnel vision- field of vision is constricted.
- Nausea
- Feeling of warmth
- Cold, clammy sweat
- Yawning
- Blurred vision

During a vasovagal syncope episode, bystanders may notice:
- Jerky, abnormal movements
- A slow, weak pulse
- Dilated pupils

Recovery after a vasovagal episode begins soon after fainting, generally in less than a minute. However, standing up too soon after fainting increases the risk of fainting again.

Chapter 1: When Things Fell Apart

"Misery won't touch you gentle. It always leaves its thumbprints on you; sometimes misery leaves them for others to see, sometimes for nobody but you to know of." -Edwidge Danticat, The Farming of Bones

    I am an average working mother who has a four-year degree. I chose marriage and motherhood, which altered my career path as this choice does for so many women. I sought other ways to make a living. I realized shortly after working in my career field that I wanted more flexibility in my future to be able to spend time with my children, so I became a licensed cosmetologist several years after graduating from college. I spent roughly two years working part-time jobs while completing a fifteen hundred hour North Carolina state mandated cosmetology curriculum. Subsequently, I went on to pass the state's written and practical exams just a few months after my daughter was born via C- section. I was pressing my way forward as I had been accustomed to doing to achieve my goals regardless of the challenges. I quickly used my new license to gain employment and additional income for our household. Professionally things started to turn around for me. I landed a job with local school system as a Tutor and later was hired to work as a lead teacher for an after-school program.

However, I had been trying for years to navigate my way though a broken healthcare system. I had gone through periods with and without health insurance coverage for myself due to affordability. Prior to the Affordable Healthcare Act, whenever I did have insurance coverage, my preexisting conditions were not covered. Because I had not maintained coverage consistently without any lapses, I would have to wait up to twelve months before my insurance company would cover any expenses related to my preexisting condition, which was Asthma. As a result, I combated uncontrolled asthma symptoms with inadequate health coverage. Unfortunately, the hormones from pregnancy triggered a dramatic increase in the intensity of the attacks that I had between 2008 and 2010. These flares were often treated in the ER where I was patched up and sent on my way. Many times the emergency room was my only resort due to finances; I was the working poor. I had insurance that did not cover my preexisting condition and when I had extreme exacerbations of my asthma symptoms I had to seek immediate treatment. I found a local doctor's office who allowed me to pay for medical treatment based upon my income and they would offer me a bevy of free samples of certain medications that were not covered by insurance to help manage my symptoms. During that time I made too much money to receive any type of public assistance to help me with my medical coverage. I fell into the abyss of the middle class segment who could not really afford adequate health insurance premiums. We had tried to maintain it, but our payments were just as much as our mortgage and daycare bills at the time. We simply could not afford our basic needs along with the hefty premiums.

Despite all of that I felt compelled to give 110% to my job. I am like that about most things that I pursue in my professional life, sometimes to my detriment. I came down with at a bout of bronchitis but as an overachiever, I did not take off from work to recover. In fact, I loaded up the cold passenger bus early on the morning of Saturday, February 20, 2010 venturing to a training conference in Charlotte, NC. I traveled with all of my medications in hand yet, I felt completely exhausted. I knew that I should have stayed home and rested and let the medication and antibiotics have time to work. I know it was important to give my body time to rest and recover but that is not a mantra by which I abide. I felt like I had to go to work. I would rest some other time. Too many people were depending on me to be "there."

The following Monday, I was already feeling a little off. I went to the doctor's office and was told my blood pressure was a slightly high. They were sure it was due to the short course of steroids I was taking as part of my treatment for the bronchitis and asthma attack I'd had the previous week. By Tuesday afternoon, I was feeling more jittery than usual, and by that evening I didn't feel quite like myself at all. I was still trying to shrug it all off. The steroids were tapering off out my system and other than the asthma, I was pretty healthy. I was surrounded by kids at work as a tutor in the mornings and as a lead instructor for an after- school program in the afternoons. Even some of the kids I worked with couldn't keep up with me. I was in relatively good shape; I had been working out regularly, watching what I ate, and had just about lost most of the baby weight from both of my children who were only seventeen months apart. However, this episode was different. The jitters didn't go away. In fact something went very wrong, terribly wrong.

Publisher comments: At this point you can see the editor flow but I ask the editor not to highlight corrections and move swiftly through the manuscript. It is much easier for the second editor to flow without having to see all these changes.

At the time, I was working two part time jobs. I returned home one evening around eight not feeling well. I went to tuck my small children in with my husband. The kids said their bedtime prayers. I walked in and knelt down beside my husband. I opened my mouth to talk and nothing came out. My mouth just clicked open and shut like a wind-up toy. I slowly got up, not wanting to alarm anyone. I was shocked and confused about the way I was feeling. I walked into living room to lie down on the couch. When my husband came out the children's bedroom he looked over at me and saw the tears streaming down my slightly twisted face. He said, "Baby, what's wrong?" I then stuttered, "I ccann't tttaallk." My husband noticed I was shaking all over and that my face was twisted to the left. He also noticed the left side of my body appeared to be weak.

    I have never been at a loss for words. My husband was immediately alarmed at my demeanor. He called his parents who only live a few houses up the street. They remained with the children while he took me to the ER. Upon arrival, my husband expressed his concern. He thought I may be having a stroke. The triage nurse said responded, "Oh, I don't think so. I am pretty sure it's anxiety." They proceeded to treat me for an anxiety attack and sent me home. Ironically, my husband was working in the mental health field at the time and knew what anxiety looked like. This was different. He knew something else was wrong.

    By Friday, my situation had deteriorated and I began having difficulty walking and dressing myself as well as speaking. My husband and my mother decided to take me to a larger facility in another city. I was immediately admitted under the suspicion of a stroke and placed under observation in the cardiac unit where they promptly began running tests to check my heart. They also consulted with Neurology who ran tests to see if there was any brain damage or lesions. I started to have seizure-like episodes with uncontrollable jerking. The episodes would last anywhere from 20 to 45 minutes at a time. The medical team quickly ruled out clinical seizures. The test for seizures was very unpleasant. They exfoliated my scalp in at least 20 different locations and attached electrodes to it. A harness was placed around my head to prevent movement while I looked at a series of flashing lights, which caused me to jerk and twitch even more. I began to cry during the test. I just wanted it to be over. I felt as if I had been placed in a horrible parallel dimension where I was being tortured and no one was going to make it stop. After almost two long, emotionally grueling days of testing, tears, and being stared at by clinical teams in sterile white coats, no one, I mean NO ONE, knew what was wrong with me.

I was dumbfounded! I felt like a broken computer whose hard drive had a meltdown and short-circuited. Nothing was working right properly. The head neurologist said, "We are not really sure at this time what is causing your symptoms, Mrs. Chubbs. However, we will have to discharge you at this time since we have found nothing about your condition to be life-threatening." Part of me was relieved that I was not dying but part of me felt terrified because I was stepping into the deep dark abyss of the unknown. I was sent home with a walker because I was still too weak and unbalanced to walk on my own. I was stuttering when I talked. I was jerking and shaking constantly. My head was aching like I'd been hit in the back of it. I was frightened. I had every right to be…who wants to face the boogeyman…no one!

Chapter 2: What's Happening to Me?

"I don't think that we're meant to understand it all the time. I think that sometimes we just have to have faith." -Nicholas Sparks, A Walk to Remember

Back at home, my husband put a post or two on Facebook informing everyone of my condition. He wanted everyone to know that I had not had a stroke and was resting at home. He let me listen to several heartfelt messages and prayers left for me on his voicemail. The voice messages encouraged me and gave me some comfort. My immediate family was there to welcome me home. My mother-in-law had even made baked salmon for me, which is one of my favorites. Unfortunately, I couldn't even finish eating. I was starting to shake badly. My mother helped me up from the table and I went to lie down for a while. Then some of the deaconesses and ministers came over from the church to which I belonged at the time. They wanted to pray for me. It was the first time I really sensed a very powerful presence of God in my life. Somehow, I knew that this journey that I was embarking on would be a catalyst to help others at some point in the future. I knew that this journey was not going to be just for me alone but somehow for others.

What To Do When The Storm Comes

They prayed with my mother as well as with my husband. My mother was a little more reluctant than my husband; her faith was profoundly shaken by my ordeal. I am her firstborn and oldest of three. I have always been her rock and she has been mine for so many years. This journey was going to be yet another trial for our family to go through. But this test would be the toughest yet.

If I thought my faith had been tested before, I had not seen anything thus far. Most of us take for granted everyday tasks like being able to walk, talk and move freely. It was now a challenge for me to accomplish these simple tasks, these gifts that God has given many of us that I had taken for granted. My family lives in a small, single-story, two bedroom home. The distance from my sofa in my living room to my bathroom is less than twenty feet. During my first few weeks back home it took me more than a minute and a half to get from the sofa to the restroom with a walker. When I had to actually bathe myself and get dressed I was exhausted afterward. I would shake and would have to lie down and take a nap after each bath.

However, rest was far from my reality. In the early onset of this disorder, as the weeks passed through the months of March and April of 2010, I had trouble sleeping. Many times I would roll over and wake up screaming at my husband, "Chucky, my head, my head, it hurts. I need Tylenol. I need something to make it stop!!" I would clasp my hands over the back of my head as if to apply pressure to an open wound. I was in pain! I wanted it to stop! Eventually an hour later it would subside.

At night, as I tried to go to sleep, I again felt the tingling and numbness on the left side of my body and a burning sensation in my scalp. What was happening to me? I felt a wave come over my body as if an electrical current was pulsing through my very being. My breathing became shallow. Then came again, the jerking, the violent jerking! Was I having a seizure? I really didn't know. I wanted to tell my husband what I was feeling. A sense of discouragement came over me as I felt my mouth tighten up. I tried to move my mouth and nothing came out. The tension prevailed as the spasms took hold of my body.

My husband called out "Tootie, can you hear me? Baby, squeeze my hand if you can hear me." I could hear him. Hearing is the one thing that always functions if all else fails. It was absolutely frightening. Imagine not being able to communicate but being able to hear the surrounding noises. This is what my world is like. All of this took place as he dialed 911, just as he has countless times since. We have had many sleepless nights. He dreaded calling my mother. He was in constant fear that others would hold him responsible for any harm that might possibly result from one of these attacks. Prior to receiving any diagnosis the fear of the unknown was taking on a life of its own. Fear can create a domino effect on everyone that is involved. For my husband the brunt of it fell upon him since he was my primary caregiver, the first one to be a witness to the chaotic episodes that would ensue. That in itself was a horrible burden to have and contend with on a fairly frequent basis for anyone, especially the man I so dearly love.

Through the roller coaster rides of falling spells, pseudo seizures, ambulance rides and doctors visits, I saw God strengthening not only me, but also my marriage. Not every marriage is made to withstand the bad times, but our marriage actually grew stronger through the adversity. I saw God's love manifesting itself through our struggle. I knew that somehow through all of this he was going to use this trial as a way for us to help others in the future that may have to endure a hardship and be able to still stand on the word of God in the midst of the storm. God helped us find peace in prayers and within each other. Not that every day was a sunny day, but with faith we knew that we would be able to endure. Hebrews 11:1 says "Now faith is the substance of things hoped for, the evidence of things not seen." Even though there were many days that it seemed like we were going to break from the pressure that was placed on our family from this ever present battle, God kept us.

I returned to the same medical facility that previously admitted me for a follow-up medical evaluation. The head neurologist with her heavy demeaning accent said, "We can't find anything wrong with you. We can keep giving you tests but who is going to pay for it?" Needless to say, I could only get what my insurance would pay for and I didn't have anything but emergency Medicaid at the time. I was upset and angry. Since when, did human suffering have a price tag? I wonder how many other Americans whom did not have the finances to find out what's wrong with them felt stuck! Stuck with being sick, mistreated, and misdiagnosed by a system that has become largely impractical.

We have become a society grossly inhabited by insurance companies who dictate who gets what type of treatment and for how long. In addition to all of this, many physicians have adopted this disconnected mindset. I long for the days where physicians actually upheld the oath to serve. Now, many of us are left to deal with a system that has facilitated the growth of uncaring practitioners who took a Hippocratic Oath. They have just turned out to be by large in part mostly hypocrites. Yes, we still have a consortium of doctors who will go above the call of duty to meet our needs and listen to our concerns, but they are diamonds in the rough.

My husband and I left that appointment feeling dejected and less hopeful for the future. I was tearful and depressed with no diagnosis. The staff neurologist had prescribed me a medication that caused me to gain over thirty pounds in less than three months. This just added insult to injury. Not only could I barely get around now, I also had to bear the burden of the extra pounds to go along with it. I quickly gathered my mind and worked on changing my diet and trying to slowly rehabilitate myself. I researched my symptoms. I still had to find a way to stay encouraged during this newfound hardship in my life.

I recall an occasion in 2012, when EMS responders came to my residence after I had fallen. I had been folding laundry in my living room when I felt myself getting weak. I attempted to make my way from the back side of our sofa to sit down but fell before I could make it. It was the middle of the week and EMS arrived at my home at 9:30 that evening. I could hear, feel, and see everything that was going on around me but I couldn't move or talk. These insensitive individuals had already come up with their own scenario. They checked my blood sugar and determined it was low. They then asked my husband, "Did she eat today?" He quickly responded, "Yes". They immediately considered my lack of response to them as refusal rather than inability and so used an ammonia break under my nose.

They got a response: fear and tears! My body jumped up a little from the floor as a natural response to a stimulus and I cried. I still could not talk or move deliberately. One EMS responder said, "You can stop now and talk to us." I was so angry! I wanted to get up but I couldn't. I wanted to talk but I couldn't! Oh, the torture didn't stop there. It was only the beginning. The worst part was the ride in the ambulance. My husband had to drive separately and take the kids to his parents' house. My family would meet me at our local emergency room. I couldn't object to riding with EMS because I couldn't talk. Once we were inside the ambulance, the male responder said to me in a taunting voice, "If you don't stop playing around I will do another ammonia break!" I felt like a trapped animal. I was strapped to a gurney in the back of an ambulance with someone who thought I was putting on an overdramatic performance. He said, "Did your husband find out something he didn't like? Did you just want a break from your family?"

I prayed to God in that moment to give me the strength to talk. He did. It was a very strong stutter at first and it started out as, "Wwhaat isss yyour nnname?" The EMS responder seemed taken aback. I repeated it again, "Wwhat iss yyour nnname?" He told me his name. Then my words came easier. I proceeded to tell him when the attacks happened. During the course of the ambulance ride, which was approximately forty five minutes after I had fallen at my residence, my speech and motor function remained impaired and it was a challenge to communicate. "What you were just doing to me I perceived as threats and not as a means of strong persuasion to gain my cooperation", I said. He quickly realized his gross error in judgment and of his treatment of me and repeatedly apologized. I could have taken my complaint further, and should have, but I didn't. The things I have been through dealing with an unknown illness and medical professionals who have never seen or treated someone in my predicament are astonishing! Once I arrived at the emergency room my emotions were still wound up.

Once I saw my husband I expressed my anger and frustration over what had happened. I told him to never leave me alone with EMS responders again! I felt so helpless, like they could do anything to me and I was defenseless. However, something in my spirit brought me to a place of calm. The EMS responder continued to apologize for what happened and ultimately forgiveness and mercy prevailed. My anger began to subside and as my situation improved the medical staff discharged me and sent me home. That situation was a lesson learned for me and my husband to be more attentive to what medical staff and personnel are doing during treatment to your loved ones and to question if the treatment is necessary. Needless to say, I was leery about going on any ambulance rides after that incident. My husband only called for help if my jerking or pseudo seizure episodes did not subside on their own in a rapid manner.

Through my own willfulness, after about two months, I made an attempt to go back to work. My parents always had a strong work ethic. Growing up in a single parent home for half of my life, I always felt like failure was not an option. I watched my mother go to work on days even when she didn't feel like it to provide for our family. Who was I to complain about my predicament? I proceeded to put on a brave face and I got in my car and drove to work. I went back to my part-time job as a reading and language tutor. I had to resign from my lead teacher position from the after-school program because I was not well enough to do both. There were times that I was at work and I would start shaking so badly that my husband or father-in-law would have to pick me up. Just like every other challenge I have faced in my life, I was determined to press forward and continue to show up to work as much as possible. I was not going to give up. I was not going to quit! Quitting is not part of my vocabulary. Ecclesiastes 9:11 says,

What To Do When The Storm Comes

"For the race is not given to the swift, but to the one who endures"! I had made up my mind that I had to keep moving because I have a son and a daughter to live for and they are counting on me to be their mother.

Eventually, it seemed like my symptoms started to get better after being home for about two months. Gradually I went back to what I would usually do and pushed myself to do more as I saw improvement over the following months. I went back to cosmetology and picked up a few clients. I still had good and bad days. There were days that I would wake up and my legs would not move or I would automatically start jerking at the startling sound of the blaring alarm clock. It was as if my body was constantly in a state of shock, like I was still slowly recovering from a traumatic experience from some undetermined culprit.

I attribute my resilient sprit to that of my mother, whom I always saw work hard and not complain when trying to provide for my brothers and me during my teenage years. I was determined to still contribute to my household financially. I decided to focus my energy into making jewelry to sell at a local craft fair in the spring of 2010. It was a challenge for me to steady my hands at times to create the intricate patterns for the necklaces, bracelets, and earrings. It required a lot of wiring and stringing, but I did it. I continued to make jewelry, on and off for about four hours while at the fair. My mother and mother-in-law stayed with me and kept a watchful eye over me to make sure I was ok since I was still shaking from time to time.

The following spring, on April 16 2011, I was at the same local craft fair selling my jewelry on an extremely windy Saturday morning. My husband was participating in the local bar-b-que cook-off that was part of the fair activities that day. The abnormally windy weather would lead to an event that I would not forget. The town officials eventually shut down the event early due to inclement weather, which in my case triggers symptoms. I quickly gathered up my things and packed them away and had my babysitter meet me at the salon that I was in front of at the time.

We were getting ready to go uptown when the lady who worked across the street at the pizza parlor asked me to do her hair. I decided to stay at the salon and that made the difference between being in harm's way and being safe. An EF-3 tornado had touched down in our area of Sanford, NC. I could see the tornado in the distance. I was terrified for myself and my children. We hid in the bathroom of the salon which was covered in big glass windows and mirrors. I told, my children, "God will keep us safe from danger. God will make everything ok." I told them to curl up in a ball on the floor and protect the backs of their heads. All the while we were praying for God to "keep us covered and to keep us safe from any hurt, harm, or danger, seen or unforeseen. In the name of the Father, in the name of the Son, and in the name of the blessed Holy Spirit." My children were only three and two years old at the time. They were scared but they were comforted in knowing that God was going to keep us safe in the midst of the storm!

Finally, we heard a tap on the front door of the salon; it was my husband. He'd come to get all of us out of there. He had been down the street at the local elementary school during the storm. Just before he arrived, we were still in the salon bathroom, surrounded by the large glass mirrors. We took our babysitter home in heavy wind and rain and then we finally returned home after running into a lot of blocked roads. We all stayed at my in- laws home and used a generator.

Unfortunately, all the activity of the day proved to be too much for me. As we were sitting in the darkness of the stormy night, the wind continued to howl. The rain continued to pour down. We sat in silence. In the middle of the storm, I sat in a blue cushioned rocking chair attempting to relax. My father- in-law was sitting in the room with me. My husband had left out to try to find gas for the generator. I began to shake in the darkness. My face began to pull to the left side. I slowly felt an unsettling feeling creep over me the same feeling I got when I knew that an episode was beginning to ensue. I wanted to talk. I attempted to tell my father in- law that I was not feeling well but my mouth would not open at all to form any word. In the still quietness, the phone rang and my father-in-law said, "Tootie, answer the phone!" Having received no response he repeated it again. Finally, he sighed deeply and got up to answer the phone. All the while I was sitting in the chair shaking even more. Tears ran down my cheek. The night had fallen. The darkness camouflaged the storm. It was happening right there under our noses. Something more deadly and treacherous was stirring up in the sky.

I suddenly began to jerk back and forth in the chair while producing loud hiccup like noises. I continued until I'd slid completely onto the floor. My mother-in-law had come from the back room once my father-in-law realized that I was in trouble. Darkness distorted their vision but not their perception of sound. I knew what was going on and what was getting ready to happen. I just knew that I was going to need help. They placed a pillow under my head and tried to call my husband but all the signals were still busy because of the tornado that was still running rampant throughout North Carolina. My jerking seizure spells lasted for over an hour before dissipating. Under normal circumstances my family would have called an ambulance for me but we knew that EMS was already overwhelmed. It would be pointless to call after such a devastating day.

As the spell subsided, I began to get the feeling back in my lower extremities. My husband had returned home and, along with my mother-in-law, helped me onto my feet. I slowly dragged my left side down the hallway to the restroom where they helped me onto the commode to urinate. My body was still was in shock from the attack. It took me almost ten minutes just to eliminate urine. I was scared. Something was horribly wrong with me. I'd been told me that I did not have Multiple Sclerosis or some other type of life-threatening disease. But in that very moment I couldn't help but realize I was having some serious doubts about the actual state of my health and lack of a proper diagnosis. There I was, a grown woman, sitting in the bathroom under the supervision of two adults.

The next morning, I was extremely tired and lethargic from the attack. However, I was grateful that God had spared our lives and our homes from the tornado. Everything else around us was in shambles. We learned that the tornado that hit our area had sustained winds of 140-160 mph. I thank God for His protection and covering. Even though I had a

Finding Strength Through Adversity

rough night it could have been much worse.

I recall another incident when I was on my way to pick up my children from daycare. They were only going part-time to keep the costs down. I was leaving work to pick them up. I started to feel a little disoriented as I came near the street I was turning on. Just as I pulled up into the daycare driveway and placed my car in park, I felt a pseudo seizure began to take place. According to the doctors I didn't have seizures. The sitter for my children opened the door of her residence after she noticed that I had been outside about five minutes past my children's normal pickup time. Then she went back inside and peeked at me through her screen door. She later, told me that she thought that I was on the phone. I had been shaking so violently I couldn't use my cell phone to call for help. I did not lose consciousness, but I was not able to talk or move freely. After about ten more minutes, she finally came over to the car. She then saw the tears rolling down my face and me jerking in the driver's seat and called for help. I was frightened as I sat in the car alone; sitting in my car waiting for someone to realize that I needed help. This was a constant fear during this point in my life. I had to live with knowing something was wrong with me, but not knowing how to manage it. Most of my immediate family knew something was wrong as well. Every time I left home I was taking a chance of something happening. I thank God for his covering and protection over my life. In all actuality all of us are at risk of hurt, harm or danger everyday; however, he sees fit to keep us here another day!

The worst episode occurred while my kids were awake. They were only four and five years old. I was walking in the living room and I simply fell to the floor. This has happened more than 15 times over four years. My children watched my husband kneel down beside me trying to get me to communicate with him. Whenever I have a migraine attack, I am often unable to communicate at all. I can hear everything. I feel everything. But I cannot respond, which is absolutely frightening. The kids were looking at me lying there on the floor. My son said, "Daddy is Mommy dead?" I heard my husband trying to keep his composure. He replied, "Son, no, your Mommy is not dead. She is ok." I started to cry. It's amazing that no matter what my tears still work. I questioned in that moment whether or not I was dying. In 2011, I still had not been diagnosed. I was still fighting an unforeseen adversary, who clearly had the upper hand.

Chapter 3: Fighting to Find Myself

"You have set yourselves a difficult task, but you will succeed if you persevere, and you will find a joy in overcoming obstacles. Remember, no effort that we make to attain something beautiful is ever lost. What I am looking for is not out there, it is in me." — Helen Keller

On a warm, breezy sunny day in April 2012, we took a family trip to Asheboro Zoo. It was an unusual day for me because I was able to enjoy the entire trip without any setbacks. We barely used the trolley that shuttled people from one destination to the next. We didn't want to miss anything. I thank God for days like this. There were days that seemed as though all the suffering and the dysfunction were merely a misunderstanding. All was well again with me and my family. It seemed like I was having more good days than bad days and I was milking it for all that it was worth. I had managed to lose a lot of the weight that I had gained from my last bout. I was feeling more optimistic about life in general. I was more willing to drive slightly longer distances to visit friends to reclaim what was left of my dying social life.

I secretly began to resent my husband for his ever-busy social life. I no longer had one. It wasn't because my husband did not want me to have one; I just merely lost the confidence to go out in general because of my unpredictable condition. Having turned down enough invitations, people simply stopped inviting me. They predicted I had some other "problems" and presented theories as to why I didn't participate in activities anymore. It was kind of sad and hurtful at times to feel left out, or even judged in some cases. They didn't understand the magnitude of my struggle. I didn't even understand the full scope of what I was struggling with.

Many do not understand what it's like to go from being the party starter to being the one outside of the party looking in through the window. I had to turn down and cancel out on so many events because I was not well enough to go. I was fearful that something would happen to me at a large event and the embarrassment and chaos that would ensue should I suffer from one of my mysterious attacks would be insurmountable. I even had someone close to me get upset because I backed out of an event that was paid for at the last minute. She did not understand that I really did not have a choice. My unpredictable symptoms flared up so awfully. I was terrified that I would not make it through the event. I couldn't deal with disappointing anyone else like that again. It took a while before I got up the nerve to try to go to another event.

My medical expenses skyrocketed from 2010 to 2013 via countless visits to the emergency room, ambulance rides for uncontrolled seizure activity, and visits to neurologists as well as other specialists, all bearing no conclusive evidence as to what was causing the massive complexities of dysfunction in my life. I found myself becoming obsessed with researching information on symptoms. I was desperate for answers. It was horrible not knew what was happening to me. I knew that I could handle whatever IT was. If only I knew what to call it One day, I found something about complex migraines. At the time I had a better job with comprehensive insurance. I took my findings to my local neurologist. He ordered new MRIs, which came back negative, and my blood work came back within normal limits. This was unexpected as my blood work was always a little wacky. I gave the doctor my medical history. I spoke of my numerous visits to the ER for my unexplained symptoms: slurred or stuttering speech, twisting of my face to the left, one sided weakness, left-sided paralysis, and violent shaking and jerking which was deemed not to be seizures. I was in desperate need of help. He did not have any answers but gave me a prescription for Verapimil, which is given to help regulate high blood pressure and to help treat migraines. I was also given a very low dose of Topamax to help with my atypical migraines and my neurological symptoms. I saw him for about a year during which there was no real improvement of my symptoms. After continuing with more late night emergency room visits for pseudo seizures and missing days from work, the severity and frequency of my symptoms increased. This included slurred speech for several days in a row and impaired motor function which required me to use a cane for assistance in late 2012 going into 2013.

    I was constantly living in fear of the next fall, the next attack, the next episode. Often times, my attack happened with little or no warning. I was getting close to the end of my rope. A local neurologist then gave me an ultimatum. He said, "Before I do anything, I want you to have a four hour long psychological screening done." I felt like I was pushed into a corner. I did not want to follow through with this. I felt like this was his way of invalidating what was going on with me. It seemed like he was saying I was crazy! I went all the way to Fayetteville, NC to a psychology clinic for a pre-evaluation to obtain approval for the actual screening. I ran into some financial issues and could not take the test as scheduled and found out that the approval was only good for one month. When I called back to reschedule they said I was not compliant and wouldn't see me. They meant that I was supposed to go in for a psychology appointment at their clinic, which I had cancelled but only because I had an emergency room visit for a seizure episode the night before. I was not able to make the one hour drive to the clinic. When I asked to leave a message with their director I was told he did not have a voicemail.

I was dumbfounded! How could a mental health clinician not have confidential voicemail? My mother is a social worker and she has a confidential voicemail. I told them they didn't have to worry about me coming to their clinic again. I had serious concerns about how they would handle my private and confidential information. I took it one step further. I called the testing facility to find out who was qualified to make referrals for testing there. The neuro-physiological screening took four hours. Much to my surprise they informed me that my neurologist could have made the referral directly to the facility for the four hour long neuro-physiological screening. It was not necessary for me to have seen a psychologist in the first place.

After this whole ordeal I felt completely let down and jaded with the medical profession. I felt like there was no help they could give me. No one knew what was wrong with me. At this point, I had stopped seeking help from neurologists. I felt like a super sleuth trying to keep journals on what may trigger my symptoms. After another visit from a pair of female EMS responders, they suggested that I have my gynecologist see if I had a hormonal imbalance. I followed their advice and had a full workup done by my OBGYN. She checked out everything, since I suffered from seizure—like episodes almost every month around my menstrual cycle, but found nothing. Sadly, on average, I took an ambulance ride every other month because of seizure activity that would not subside and required medical treatment. But during the other weeks I was going to Zumba to work out. I felt like I was getting myself back, for the most part. I found out I was vitamin D deficient. I was not missing as much work as before. I was attempting to have a social life again.

In a sense, I became my own physician. I took myself off all of the medication that the neurologist had put me on previously. I had seen no improvement so why put my liver through the process of having to detoxify my system of drugs? I tried to change my diet, exercise more, and monitor my stress level as much as possible. It all seemed to help for a time. It seemed like most of my symptoms had stabilized although I still had some episodes of jerking and fainting. Many times, the very next day, I would get up and continue on. Nevertheless, I was going on like nothing that was happening was taking its toll on me and my family. By the fall of 2013 my mother kept insisting that I find a new physician. I was still very pessimistic and reluctant but did take the time to look for a migraine headache specialist online. I found one and called to inquire about whether or not I needed a referral and what type of insurance they accepted. Everything was a green light should I need to see them in the future. It would be sooner than I expected.

I soon returned to the reality that I had not really dealt with the elephant in the room. During the beginning of the 2013 school year I realized that on top of the very atypical migraine symptoms that caused me temporary paralysis on my left side, I was actually starting to sustain some type of dysfunction. For a moment I thought it was in my head. But much to my disbelief it wasn't. I noticed that when I walked my left hand and foot curled in and under. I would become aware of it and try to straighten it out and after a few minutes of activity it would revert back. I walked but now turned inward. My fears were heightened.

What To Do When The Storm Comes

I was desperately trying not to let this enigma control my life but I really was not in charge. I was trying to regain some type of balance for my own sanity. I just wanted to feel normal. It didn't help when some family or friends around me, thought I was making things up. "It's all in your head," one might say. They thought I could control it. "You must not really be sick. They can't find anything wrong with you!" These are the things that I had to listen to and endure while trying to cope with this "bully." However, I listened to that still small voice inside of me that said, "I know that something is wrong with me. I will not rest until I get to the bottom of it! I will not accept their lack of knowledge as a reply any longer!"

I had an opportunity on January 21, 2013 to disprove my former neurologist's theory that I had some type of anxiety disorder. This is the same doctor who stated that he would not perform any further research or evaluation to clarify my exact condition until I completed a neurological - psychological examination. My husband and I decided to organize a tour to Washington, DC for the second Inaugural Address for President Barack Obama. We organized a one day trip by bus with approximately 60 other people in attendance for the trip. We traveled on the crowded Metro into

Finding Strength Through Adversity

Washington, DC to the National Monument for the main event with thousands of other participants. My mother and I were separated from the group. We had to crisscross and push through the masses to make our way back to our group. When it was time to depart from the National Mall, parts of the Metro had broken down and we became stuck in a line that did not move in either direction for over an hour. We were shoulder to shoulder with absolute strangers. If I had an anxiety or stress conversion disorder that would have been an ideal time to snap. Even my husband was starting to become unglued. The only breakdown that happened on that long day trip occurred with public transportation. It was nice to prove unfounded theories incorrect. I'd told the doctors all along, stress is a factor in all illnesses, but stress alone was not what was causing all of my problems.

Chapter 4: Regrouping

"Growth is a spiritual process, doubling back on itself, reassessing and regrouping."-Julia Margaret Cameron

I was frightened that I had suffered some type of nerve damage from all of the migraine attacks and it was somehow overlooked. I was scared. In September, I finally went to the Migraine Headache specialist in Raleigh, NC. He looked over all of my medical records and we discussed some of the things I'd researched as well and his preliminary findings. He suspected that I may have a rare migraine disorder called Hemiplegic Migraines but still needed to do more testing. He scheduled me a few weeks later to see a cardiologist for a tilt table test.

I remember one afternoon, while walking to my car at the end of the day, I was stopped by one of the tutors at my job. She told me that she admired me because of my faith. I was taken aback. She said, "You have really helped to increase my faith in God just by watching you and how you have carried yourself. I have seen you come to work on days that you clearly did not feel well. Sometimes you were walking with a cane. You still find a way to be pleasant and to smile and to treat others with kindness." I told her, "Thank you!" and proceeded to share with her, "I am aware other people who are watching me. Since I call myself a Christian, it will benefit no one for me to mope and complain. I choose to be careful how I treat others because they are not to blame for my misfortune. It's not their fault, this has happened to me. So, if God has allowed my circumstances to help bring someone closer to him then so be it. It's worth it!" I gave her a hug. I wiped a few happy tears from my face before I drove home. But my faith would be tested even further.

Unfortunately, in mid October of 2013, before I could even have the tilt table test done, I became very sick. The first red flag that I was heading into a downward spiral was that I was not feeling well right around lunch time at work. I was sitting in the cafeteria with my co-workers and we were eating and supervising all of the children during lunch. I proceeded to get up to throw away some trash. As I headed back towards the table my eyes rolled back and my knees buckled. I hit the cafeteria floor. I was thinking, "Dear Lord, not again." This had happened to me once before the previous year in a Kindergarten classroom. I proceeded to jerk and shake on the cafeteria floor in a seizure-like manner. I was not able to talk to anyone for a few minutes. They called an ambulance for me and contacted my husband. I cried a little but quickly gained my composure. I knew that my body was just letting me know that I was overdoing it. I had to let some things go. Unfortunately, it was a little too late.

    I tried to return to work as I had done numerous times in the past and I proceeded to have four more falling/fainting spells within two weeks, which was extremely alarming. My doctor immediately took me out of work until we could figure out what was going on. However, I had to endure the nightmare of being transported to my local emergency room. They treated me like I had no prior knowledge about my medical history or condition. They completely ignored any information that my husband or I tried to offer them upon my admittance to the emergency room. I was infuriated. At least thirty minutes passed before I had regained my ability to speak and express myself somewhat. The on-call physician had treated me during a previous visit. She proceeded to regurgitate to me outdated information received from my neurologist. I told the physician that I had not seen that neurologist in over a year and yet she ignored me, saying instead that I have pseudo seizures and that the treatment available at the ER was not going to help me. I was angry at

Finding Strength Through Adversity

not being listened to and wished nothing more than to be released as soon as possible.

Soon after, I was able to make it to the cardiologist in Raleigh for my tilt table test. This was a turning point for my family and me. They strapped me down to the table and inserted an IV. They constantly monitored my blood pressure. The object of the test was to see if I suffered from sudden severe drops in my blood pressure, which was constantly monitored during the process. The answer was a resounding YES! I had been suffering for over four years with falling spells because I had developed a condition called Vasovagal Syncope. I had not been treated for any of this. The falls in themselves can be mistaken for seizures because all of my blood pooled in the lower half of my body and moved away from my brain. To make matters worse, I had been given medication for high blood pressure at one point, which only exacerbated my medical situation.

I was happy and frustrated all at the same time. I remember my husband starting to break down at the hospital and saying, "Now we are starting to find out part of what's wrong with her. You don't know what it's like watching someone go through this and not knowing what's wrong and not knowing how to help them!" He quickly gathered himself as he is not the type to get overly emotional. On the other hand, I will cry at commercial! I was a mix of emotions in this moment of discovery. How could I have been paying a medical professional for over a year and a half? He never once delved into why I kept having falling spells. I always seemed to appear healthy in person despite my facial tics and twitches. One thing that I have learned when it comes to one's health is just because it may look like a duck does not mean that it is one. In other words, everything is not always as it seems.

In mid September 2013, shortly after these findings, my migraine specialist said he could no longer see me. He felt like my case was far too complex. Besides the Hemiplegic Migraines, he suspected that my primary dysfunction was a movement disorder called Dystonia. He stated that he was inclined to believe this based on how I presented medically, but that he was not a movement disorder specialist. Therefore, he was going to refer my case to be further evaluated by a clinician who specialized in treating patients who may have my type of disorder in the hopes of helping me reach a more definitive conclusion. I was bummed because this particular doctor was one of the nicest and most professional that I had met thus far. I had anxiety about being transferred to a neurologist who specialized in movement disorders. I was a bit stressed that I had to travel all the way to Durham, NC to seek further evaluation. I had no choice but to go on short-term medical leave and wait for my appointment. I was officially taken out of work during the second week of November 2013. My appointment with the new doctor would not be until January. The waiting was going to be pure agony.

We were entering into the holiday season, a time of joy and merriment. Instead, it was a time of anxiety and ambiguity for me. I was anxious to see if this new doctor would finally hold some magical key to unlock the mystery of what had been plaguing me all these years. The possibility to have my symptoms validated as real, and not imagined, and the opportunity to give a name to the primary cause for all of the irregular movement and activity that my body had to contend with, filled me with hope for a brighter day to come. No one wants to have something wrong with them. I just wanted to be able to move on with my life and start a new chapter. I could handle whatever was wrong; I just wanted to know exactly what it was.

Chapter 5: Hitting Rock Bottom

"You may encounter many defeats, but you must not be defeated. In fact, it may be necessary to encounter the defeats, so you can know who you are, what you can rise from, how you can still come out of it." — Maya Angelou

I had been sitting at home on the couch for at least two months and was very weak. I was tired from the entire physical trauma. I was tired from all of the migraine attacks. The ticking, jerking, and shaking were more than enough for anyone to deal with. We all agreed: I would not drive for over two and a half months. I did not drive at all. I was taken everywhere. I needed someone to go with me everywhere, which fell mainly to my father in-law. I felt like I was on house arrest for a crime that I did not commit.

It was after January 2014 before I got to meet with the movement disorder neurologist. He did a preliminary evaluation, checking my reflexes and reviewing my referring physician's notes. He also reviewed the medical information that I provided him. He said that he wanted to run some genetic testing blood work and that if it came back negative it would not change his overall diagnosis, if he were to have one. He did, however, order for

Finding Strength Through Adversity

me to have a very extensive physical abilities test done in Durham, NC. Basically, what that meant was more waiting. I had to wait another month for the test to take place.

Finally, the day arrived for me to take the abilities test in Durham. It was a rather dreary day. In fact, there was a call for snow that afternoon. I had just recently reclaimed my driving privileges to try and ease the burden of my family having to transport me everywhere. I drove half way to my appointment, about thirty-five minutes of winding back country roads to the main highway and met my mother in Cary, NC. She drove the remaining forty-five minutes to my appointment in Durham. I had prepared for this test by packing some snacks for the both of us since I knew it would be a while. Although I had been dealing with this mystery illness for four years, I was still nervous as I did not know what to expect. I did not know what this test was going to prove or disprove. I just did not want to be made to look like a fool again, just to have the end result tell me that I am "fine", that I am "normal", especially since nothing about my life for the past four years had been normal.

No physician had ever bothered to send me for an evaluation. They never tried to see how I actually functioned under pressure or while performing a specific task. Most of them made knee jerk assessments on my suffering. Based on a thirty minute appointment, they assumed that I was perfectly capable and fully functional. I have spent so much money and driven so many miles over the years to see different practitioners only to leave feeling empty and without answers. I arrived at this facility early for my appointment. We came through the wrong entrance which was artfully tailored for children with wonderfully colorful murals and designs to detract from what the facility's real purpose. I was redirected down the hallway of this physical therapy establishment. We saw children that were just learning to walk. There were people from all spans of life, from young to old. The children touched me. Many of them were born with some type of illness or dysfunction that hindered their ability to move freely. It was all they had ever known. Despite circumstances out of their control, they spoke and smiled and waved hello. They were completely innocent and still found a way to be happy.

Even now, it amazes me how many individuals go about their day with their faces all wrinkled up with sour dispositions. Their issues are far less challenging on a day-to-day basis. If only we could be more like those children that I saw who found a way to smile despite their daily struggles and hardships that were permanent; their struggles were not temporary, like many trials that the average person faces. I kept all this in mind during the tough days. Despite what I may be going through, I can smile and be pleasant to other people. I will not let this get the best of me!

After waiting for about twenty minutes I met this nice middle--aged woman who was about average height with a pretty gray bob and blue eyes. She told me that she would be evaluating me for the afternoon. We walked back to her area and sat down. She looked at me. She did not know what to expect. Clearly she was expecting something different. While we were sitting and talking, everything appeared to be normal. She took my blood pressure and told me it was a little high. I told her it must be my nerves.

She informed me that, the testing was going to take a couple of hours and said she would give me breaks as needed. So we began. She asked me to perform a task: hold up one leg and keep her from pushing it down. I proceeded to do it with my right leg, my dominant side, and was successful. She then asked me to do the same task with my left leg, which was my affected side. It was unsuccessful. She had me perform similar tests with my right and left arms and my left side always failed. We went on to more advanced testing. She had me stand up and balance on my right leg and I was able to do that for almost forty seconds. She had me do the same on my left side. I was only able to balance for about eighteen seconds. Everything was definitely signifying that my left side was weaker.

Then the testing became more difficult and infuriating. I had to play what appeared to be a board game. However, I would call it a more sinister edition of Trouble. The board looked like a game of checkers except all the pieces were red. The object of this activity was for me to pick up one piece with my right hand and flip it over. Then I had to place it facing down with the left. There were four rows with approximately twelve pieces in each row. The activity had to be repeated four times. In addition to this these activities were being timed. I think I had less than three minutes to complete the task. Needless to say, this is when her observations about my abilities became drastically different. While performing the task on the second try she noticed that my left hand began to curl up and that my face began to twitch on the left side. On the third try she noticed the same symptoms. My speech began to slur. I had slight jerking of my head to the left as well. By the fourth try, I could barely finish the task and was shaking quite noticeably all over and was barely able to complete the task at hand.

This pattern continued as she gave me more similar standardized tests. Somehow, during my frustrations she assured me that this information would be extremely useful for my neurologist to see. She continued to say, "No doctor has four hours to spend with you to see how every day activities would affect you." She added, "Besides, this is standardized and this measures how you would actually function under normal circumstances in a working environment." I was relieved that finally, for once, it wouldn't just be my point of view but someone's subjective and professional point of view about how difficult things really are for me daily. She also reassured me that even though I may not be thrilled about using a cane at the age of thirty- three, it was necessary. I was a fall risk. My left side was clearly weaker than my right side. She said, "Sure you can walk without it. You will cause undue strain on your back. It will tire you out. You will be able to walk for longer without the risk of falling if you use one." She later revealed to me that the doctors' notes stated that my physical function was fairly altered. Upon first meeting with me, I appeared to be fairly normal to her just based on sitting and talking. I seemed "normal" and then she saw firsthand how not "normal" my symptoms were. She said, "Well, if all else fails you can maybe write a book about all of this crazy stuff that's been happening to you all this time." I said, "I may just do that."

I had to embrace the fact that I would have to have a walking companion. I would also have the social stigma attached to it. People say the craziest things to me like, "You know you are too young to have that." They would ask, "Did someone push you down some stairs?" It's hard to deal with other people's ignorance. I have learned to deal with it by having an abundance of grace and humility in my heart. People fear what they don't understand.

The hardest thing about being diagnosed with a disorder is trying to justify it to others. In my case, I look normal for the most part. Normal looks, average build, and average weight. I just don't look like anything should be wrong with me. I say "I don't feel well" or "my legs won't move" and some perceive this as an attention-seeking behavior. Others may see it as an attempt for me to get out of doing work by being "lazy." This all can be hurtful. I have always been a hard worker. I started babysitting at the age of ten because I wanted my own money. In college, I worked a minimum of two jobs at any given time just to pay for my own expenses. I even occasionally helped my mom with bills since she was a single parent. I have always been accustomed to being helpful to others. I was not accustomed to not being the one who needs help. I was not sure how to deal with these emotions at all.

In February 2014, just days away from my 34th birthday, I was a bit depressed and didn't feel much like celebrating. I still was not back at work. I had to constantly stay on top of doctors to keep my paper work straight for my short term disability so that I could maintain my measly income and, more important, the health insurance that I so desperately needed. I spent most of my days at home watching television; my favorite channels were Food Network and E!. I had become disconnected from everything.

Since I had been home, very few people had actually called or come by to visit and see how I was actually doing. I felt invisible. I felt like everyone had forgotten about me. I will say that a few faithful elderly women, whom I love dearly, would call me periodically to see if I needed anything. I guess I could blame myself to a degree. It's not like I put on social media that I was taken out of work due to illness and that I didn't know if

What To Do When The Storm Comes

or when I could go back.

In fact, despite what little information most people knew about me I would much rather be in a position to be of help than to be the one who is helped. Most of the people where I lived knew me only through my involvement in church and the local community, but they did not know the true essence of me. I am a relatively free spirit. This was a very awkward circumstance for me as I am accustomed to getting things done at a moment's notice rather than having to wait on others. But due to my unpredictable health, I had been subjugated to waiting on other people just to go to the store to get milk. I was beyond frustrated. I was not allowed to drive and I was not allowed to walk for long distances without the aid of a cane. My husband kept asking, "What do you want to do for your birthday?" I'd always reply, "Everything that I want to do that's fun I am not able to do, so I am really not that interested." I was just not at a place where I felt like celebrating.

March 2014 was a turning point for me. My husband lost a dear uncle on Friday March 14, 2014, the night before our daughter turned six. My children were recovering from menacing stomach flu and I was just coming down with it. There was an overall heaviness in the atmosphere. My stress level was extremely high from trying to be stable and supportive not only for my husband, but also for my mother in-law. I had been helping her with different errands related to the funeral during the week while trying to recover from the stomach flu.

Tuesday night, I had a relatively bad attack with violent jerking. My husband urged me to call my neurologist. I called and spoke with his nurse the next day to see if they had gotten my results back yet. She called me back on Thursday morning right before we were leaving to go to the funeral. My phone rang and answered "Hello." She said, "Natalie all of your blood work came back normal for the genetic testing. On the other hand, your physical therapy assessment states that you are disabled." When I heard the words, "you are disabled" I stopped breathing for a moment. I simply responded, "thank you for calling me." We scheduled a follow up visit a week and a half from that day. Of course I did not say a word to my husband because it was not the time or the place. I continued to get dressed as if the conversation that I'd just had did not even take place. I put on my black dress and my pink and green floral statement necklace and earrings. My children and I waited for my mother to come. We were all riding together. Once we were in the car and on our way to the service I told her. She said "It will be ok. Disability doesn't mean that you can't do anything. What is means is you have to find some other options." As the day progressed and I sat through the service, I pondered over the course that my life was taking. In fact, I was so distracted that I forgot to put the cap on my engine after I'd put more oil in my motor. I drove for thirty minutes that way and almost messed up my car.

Once we had driven back from Fayetteville I realized my error. My mother and I sat together at the repast at my church. By this time the day's activities had started to take its toll on me. I began to shake and walk very slowly and became lightheaded. I didn't want everyone looking at me. A lot of the people there were foreign to me and unfamiliar with my symptoms. My mother walked with me outside to my car and I took a Lorazepam and sat in the car for a little while until my speech and my symptoms returned back to normal. My mother played as my spokesperson explaining to those who showed concern about what was going on with me in general. I still had not been given an official diagnosis nor had I shared the fact that I had been told that I have a disability.

Once I felt better and we had left the church, my mother and I went to buy another cap to put on my engine. My mother gave me a big hug before she went back to her home in Raleigh. I stayed at my in-laws house and talked with all of my husband's new-found family. I didn't want to seem anti- social. I figured even if my face was twitching, I didn't have to hide myself in a room. The fact is that if you learn not to make a big deal out of your flaws or issues, other people will learn to deal with them too and it will no longer be an issue. We often times over–emphasize our weaknesses and do not give ourselves enough credit for our strengths.

Later on in the evening after we put the children to bed, I finally told my husband about the phone call. I told him, as I had been told, "I was disabled based on my assessment." I then went on to say, "I do not know how to mentally process this information or even know what to do with it at the age of thirty-four. In my mind I can still walk. Even though it is difficult at times and I can still do things. However, I know that the truth is that my abilities wax and wane in their consistency." The one thing that still eluded me was an actual diagnosis. I desperately wanted to see my doctor to see if he had any answers for me.

The time quickly came for my appointment and inclement weather was threatening to rear its ugly head. I almost cancelled but the next appointment time would be three months away. I simply could not stand for that. I drove to Cary,

What To Do When The Storm Comes

NC where I met my mother. She picked me up and drove the remaining stretch to Durham. It seemed like we were going to be late for the appointment. I think my anxiety about the outcome had created a warped sense of time because–we actually ended up being on time for the appointment. We parked and strolled in with no snow yet in sight. We checked in with the receptionist and I waited to be called back while my mother ran back to her car to retrieve her cell phone. Just as she came back inside we were being called into the back. When the nurse weighed me, I had lost about four pounds. When she took my blood pressure, it was on the low side, which never happens. It is usually quite high and considering the situation it should have been this time as well. I was nervous. So far, so good. Finally, the doctor came back and talked with both of us.I stood as instructed and he proceeded to check my reflexes and a few simple coordination tasks. He had me go out into the hallway and walk forwards and backwards briefly. Afterwards, I sat back down on the observation table and he said, "Well, at this point it's up to you what you want to do. You know how much you want to work? Do you want to try to work or do you want to file for disability?" I said to him, "I know the report says that I am disabled but what else do I have to go on other than that?" Then he said, "Oh, I do have a diagnosis for you. You have Generalized Dystonia." I just looked at him like a deer grazing in an open pasture. I was so used to not getting results I had grown accustomed to it. It was a very awkward feeling to suddenly feel validated. I said "I have Dystonia." He said, "Yes. It is a neurological movement disorder that is very under--diagnosed. There is currently no cure for it. There are treatments to help manage the symptoms."

Something was better than knowing nothing. Now that the enemy had been identified, the battle would not be so one-sided. I no longer had to be afraid. I know what I can and can't do. I have a point of reference. My mother asked, "What is the prognosis for this condition?" The doctor responded, "I don't have a straight--forward answer because the condition itself does not have a lot of research behind it. Some people get worse. Some people get better. In some cases some have their symptoms go away completely." He explained to me the cause of my type of Dystonia had no clear known origin, or as they say in the medical field it was "idiopathic" in origin. I felt God lifting the burden of the unknown oppressor off my shoulders in that very moment. I actually started to feel liberated in my spirit knowing that if someone now asked me a question, I now had an answer!

Chapter 6: The Break Through

"Be careful in your walk, because you don't know who you are carrying with you." **-Natalie Chubbs**

I was now at a crossroads in my life where I had to figure out what I was going to do with myself, what path I was going to take. I now knew that I had the option to go on disability but I was not at a place where I was willing to accept this. I said to myself "There has got to be something else that I can do." Then I would have a bad day where nothing on my body would seem to cooperate. I'd get frustrated with myself. I was still coming to terms with the prognosis that, at least for a time, I was going to have to use a cane to walk around out in public places more often than not. I'd then have to face public speculation and judgment. I had to go to church and deal with people saying things behind my back like, "She didn't have to use that last week" or," She doesn't look sick enough to be walking with a cane."

At times I found myself getting in a rut and attempting to find things in my environment to inspire me to do more. I recall a classmate of mine from Meredith College who passed away from cystic fibrosis. She had the best spirit and the best attitude. She was the type of person who would be in the hospital trying to recover from another setback and would still insist on completing her work anyway. She had a "never quit" attitude. I always use her life as an example when I tell others why we shouldn't complain about our circumstances. We should still treat people well, despite our circumstances. I was trying to find my way. I didn't want anyone to feel sorry for me. I had a few limitations, but somehow I felt inspired to do more. I knew that I could not return to the job I once held because I could no longer drive a bus. I was ok with that. When one door closes God opens another. I wanted to show my children, "you can reinvent yourself. When things in your life don't go your way, you can still get to where you want to go."

I quickly shifted my mindset and focused on that scripture Romans 12:2 (NIV) "Do not conform to the pattern of this world, but be transformed by the renewing of your mind. Then you will be able to test and approve what God's will is-his good, pleasing and perfect will." I realized that I needed to share my story with others so that they would be encouraged to seek Gods guidance and let him be the director during the storms in their lives. He did not create us to be helpless passengers on a sinking ship. The only reason these multiple illnesses have not triumphed over me is because I

What To Do When The Storm Comes

know who I am in Christ. I did not arrive to this place overnight. This was a growth and development process. Many times God has to get us in a place where we are uncomfortable in order to get us to grow. My adversity has strengthened me and my spiritual relationship immensely. God has allowed me to become a strong beacon of hope for those who have been observing me this entire time. By his grace, I have been able to motivate others to strive for more despite their present circumstances.

As the months have progressed since my diagnosis, I have become stronger. I have become less dependent on people and more dependent on God's help. I am not as reliant on using a cane as was initially projected. I still have days that are more challenging than others. However, I do not take for granted that someone else out here in the world faces far greater challenges than I will ever have to face. I continue to thank God for what I have gained and continue to press forward. When I have days when I am feeling down, I speak over myself. I encourage you to do the same. Proverbs 8:21 (NIV) says "The tongue has the power of life and death, and those who love it will eat its fruit." Continue to speak life into your situation and have a positive attitude. It will only improve your situation! As the saying goes, "watch your words."

Chapter 7: Turning Disappointment into an opportunity- how to be your own advocate for change in your life when it comes your health.

"Life is not about finding yourself. Life is about creating yourself."-George Bernard Shaw

We have to be our own advocates and research things for ourselves. We cannot accept everything that doctors take at face value. They are just practitioners. The key word is "practicing". They have general content knowledge in various areas of study but they need guidance. You as the patient need to learn how to speak the lingo and learn how to properly communicate what is going on with **YOUR** body in terms that they understand. Research does not make you a hypochondriac, it makes you informed. Many professionals are required to meet continuing education standards, so why should we not make ourselves informed about the things that affect us as well? Who is in a better position to articulate what is going on with your body than you? If you feel like you are not getting effective treatment then take your money and time to a physician who is trained; and will listen and will get to the bottom of the issues pertaining to you and your needs.

What To Do When The Storm Comes

We have the direct power as consumers, clients, and patients to direct the path of healthcare and costs as a whole. We have to hold them accountable at the basic level of care. It's called customer or client care. If you feel like you are not being treated with the utmost respect in regards to your time and your areas of concern, you have the right to express your concerns or grievances. Many of us have gone to appointments before where we wait in the waiting room for forty minutes. We wait in a room for another thirty to forty minutes just to be transferred to yet another room. We finally see the doctor who rushes us through our concerns quickly and is out the door before ten minutes even passed. We feel cheated on our time. We feel as if we didn't come to an understanding or resolution on our plan of care or didn't have our concerns addressed. We are left with a nurse who is barely briefed on our situation to try to solve unanswered questions.

When is enough going to be enough? The buck starts and stops with you. Let your health are providers know that you are serious about your care. Ask questions about testing such as if it is necessary, and if certain medication is appropriate for your condition. When you schedule appointments ask about billing and pricing if you are in a financial bind since some offices offer better prices for clients who pay cash up front and even have a sliding scale for clients based on income. This is information that is not always advertised. As I stated earlier, "Wisdom is the principal thing. Therefore get wisdom, with all thy getting get understanding." (Proverbs 4:7)

Majority of the U.S. healthcare system is predicated on the fact that we are ignorant. We are not in a position to force the insurance companies, nor the doctors to openly compete for our patronage or participation because we have only limited information about their pricing in this free market economy. In addition to this, the insurance companies do not charge consumers fairly for similar procedures and services across the board. It is not uncommon to hear in the news about people traveling outside of the U.S to have medical procedures performed because to do so here in America would be astronomical for the identical medical procedure. Medical facilities do not charge fees in an open and transparent fashion because we as consumers have not demanded it from them by simply asking direct questions like "how am I being billed for these services or procedures?" Many times we as patients do not even see the price for the service being provided until after the service has been performed. One major factor behind our high cost here in America is that our medical pricing, aside from Medicaid and Medicare, are not regulated by our government like other developed nations. For example, here in the US, on average a patient will pay $1,185 for a Colonoscopy and in Switzerland just $655, according to the June 1, 2013 article in the NY Times, "The $2.7 Trillion Medical Bill", by Elisabeth Rosenthal.

Many of us as patients go into these situations blindly and sign on the dotted line not fully realizing what we will be paying for. Will our doctor be out-of-network even though the hospital we chose was in our network during our emergency visit? These are situations that the average American has to face and it directly affects your finances. I owe over $10,000 in medical debt from all of my ambulance rides, emergency room visits, and out of pocket expenses that I could not keep up with while I was out of work. This is just a small fraction of the reported $2.7 Trillion spent annually on overpriced healthcare related services here in the U.S. The medical industry continues to report record profits every year while, according to Mercola.com, approximately 60% of all personal bankruptcies in the United States are related to medical bills. The madness has got to come to a stop. We the people, the consumers, are the game changers who can cause the pendulum to shift in the appropriate direction. We can sound the alarm and cause the powers that be to be held accountable for decisions that they are recklessly making. We can have these corporate giants start viewing people as actual living and breathing beings and not some sort of collateral damage on a spreadsheet that has been compiled before a big staff meeting to talk about the next profit and loss statements for the company for that quarter. It's time for everyone to wake up!

The real collateral damage is the human lives that are being mishandled on a daily basis like mine. Needless suffering that follows because you fell into the wrong tax bracket is simply unacceptable. We are all human. In my opinion, all people should be afforded equal protection under the law just as it was intended under the Fourteenth Amendment based on economics. No one's medical treatment should be predicated on the fact that they can't pay as much as someone else. Nor should anyone be brought to financial ruin because of their health. All of our lives are valuable in the sight of God. These very ideals are being brought to the attention of the Supreme Court in regards to repealing the Affordable Care Act. Although the act itself may not be perfect, the intent and intention of it is to ensure that everyone has an opportunity to receive proper medical care and not be left to suffer. When did we let insurance companies start making decisions about how we live our lives? Last time I checked it takes money to stay in business. No consumers. No money. Food for thought: maybe we could just start paying the doctors' offices and hospitals for our care directly based on their customer service and performance ratings directly? We may see a difference in how we the consumers are treated.

Closing Remarks
"What's Your Plan"

*"Those who may say, 'Today or tomorrow, we will go to this city, spend a year there, carry on business and make money.' You do not even know what will happen tomorrow. What is your life? You are but a mist that appears for a little while and then vanishes. Instead you ought to say, 'If it is the Lords will, we will live and do this or that. As it is you boast or brag. All such boasting is evil."
(James 4:13-16, NIV)*

Many of us have been taught to set goals and make plans so we don't wander aimlessly throughout this life. We have been given so we can make something out of ourselves. Some of us choose to occupy our time with stacking up our bank accounts, even though we can't take it with us when we leave. Others of us spend our time trying to cover our walls with accolades and degrees that say to the world we have accomplished something. But we have not spent our time building our relationship with God.

What do you do when life does not work out the way you planned? STOP RIGHT THERE! This is where many of us have gotten it wrong when we face that road called disappointment. We forgot to consult our author and creator about his plan for us while we were making our own. Actually, the plan was never ours to begin with. The Bible says in Proverbs 3: 5-6 "Trust in the LORD with all your heart and do not lean on your own understanding. In all your ways acknowledge Him, and He will make your paths straight." He has already written our story. In Jeremiah 1:5 the word says "Before I formed you in the womb I knew you, before you were born I set you apart. " There is no need in getting down and staying there. We just need to find a quiet place and listen to God speak. He will show us where we need to go. God has already formulated a plan and a purpose for your life. He knows the REAL story of my life and yours. Sure, we have all made some mistakes and some people may have even tried to write you off because of your past. But Romans 8:28 says, (NIV) "And we know that in all things God works for the good of those who love him, who[a] have been called according to his purpose." Some people don't know all the hell that you have been through. They don't know your test and your trials. Remember that everything is working together, the good and the bad. Just know that God is perfecting you for your purpose and your test is preparation for your testimony. For in Second Corinthians 12:9-10 we are told, "My grace is sufficient for you, my strength is made perfect in weakness."(NKJV) You are simply being prepared

Finding Strength Through Adversity

for greater works!

Don't concern yourself about what man has to say about you. Concern yourself about what God says! He is the Alpha and the Omega. He knows our beginning, our middle, and our end. God never said following him would be easy. He assures us that if we let HIM use us for his glory, he will finish out our stories. Jeremiah 29:11 tells us, "For I know the thoughts that I think toward you, saith the Lord, thoughts of peace, and not of evil to give you an expected end. (KJV) The God I serve will have the final say-so. Your plans should be right now! If you haven't given your life to God, what are you waiting for? If you haven't made amends with your neighbor what are you waiting for? Don't put it off until tomorrow. Do it today! Tomorrow is not promised. AMEN!

About The Author

Natalie is the wife of Minister Harry C. Chubbs, Jr. and moth-er of Trey and Imani Chubbs, whom are both in elementary school. She is currently the Assistant Director of a 501C 3 Non-Profit organization called Transitional Rehabilitation Adjustment and Care Facility (TRAC) with her mother Theresa J. Coleman as the Executive Director and founder. Natalie is also employed as a tutor with her local school district. She is also the founder of her new business Gift of Words Consulting Firm. Gift of Words Consulting firms' goals are to motivate, train and develop others in public speaking, interviewing, literacy, and job development skills.

She is passionate about serving and helping others, which is a trait that she inherited from both her mother, a social worker, and her father, a military veteran. She is a mighty woman of God who is a prayer warrior who has developed a deep faith in the Lord through the test and trials of this life. Her personal interests and hobbies include reading and studying about history, cooking exotic food, fashion, mu-sic, art, dance, and fellowship with close friends and family.

Natalie is a graduate of Meredith College, in Raleigh, NC and holds a Bachelor of Arts in Fashion Marketing with a Minor in Management. She is also a licensed Cosmetologist. Natalie seeks to motivate and encourage others in finding their strength through their own storm and own adversity with the help of God. She believes that God uses our tests and trials as a refinement process in order to prepare us for a greater purpose that he has for each and every one of us. What to Do When the Storm Comes is her first book.

For more information about TRAC Facility go to **www.tracfacility.com**

For more information about. Gift of Words Consulting Firm go to **www.uhavethegift.com **

Made in the USA
Columbia, SC
20 January 2025